LEGENDS OF WARFARE
GROUND

M18 Hell-Cat
76 mm Gun Motor Carriage in World War II

DAVID DOYLE

SCHIFFER MILITARY
4880 Lower Valley Road   Atglen, PA 19310

Designed by Justin Watkinson
Technical Layout by Jack Chappell
Type set in Impact/Minion Pro/Univers LT Std

ISBN: 978-0-7643-5957-6
Printed in China

Published by Schiffer Publishing, Ltd.
4880 Lower Valley Road
Atglen, PA 19310
Phone: (610) 593-1777; Fax: (610) 593-2002
E-mail: Info@schifferbooks.com
www.schifferbooks.com

For our complete selection of fine books on this and related subjects, please visit our website at www.schifferbooks.com. You may also write for a free catalog.

Schiffer Publishing's titles are available at special discounts for bulk purchases for sales promotions or premiums. Special editions, including personalized covers, corporate imprints, and excerpts, can be created in large quantities for special needs. For more information, contact the publisher.

We are always looking for people to write books on new and related subjects. If you have an idea for a book, please contact us at proposals@schifferbooks.com.

Acknowledgments

As with all of my projects, this book would not have been possible without the generous help of many friends. Instrumental to the completion of this book were Tom Kailbourn, Steve Zaloga, Sean Hert, the late Jim Alexander, the late Steve Preston, Scott Taylor, Chris Hughes, Kevin Emdee, the archivists at General Motors, the staff and volunteers at the Patton Museum, and the staff at the National Archives. Most importantly, I am blessed to have the help and support of my wife, Denise, for which I am eternally grateful.

All photos are from the collection of the US National Archives and Records Administration, unless otherwise noted.

Contents

Introduction

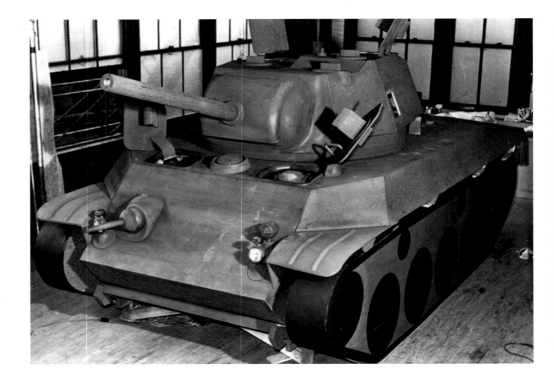

The first vehicle in the procession of tank destroyers that led to the 76 mm Gun Motor Carriage (or GMC) M18 was the 57 mm GMC T49. The T49 was conceived as a fast, highly maneuverable, lightly armored tracked vehicle with a 57 mm main gun capable of defeating the German armor of the day. Shown here is a mockup of the T49. *General Motors LLC*

In the years leading up to the US entry into World War II, the US military strategy held that enemy tanks were to be engaged not primarily by other tanks, but rather by specialized tank destroyers. Early tank destroyers were primarily towed artillery pieces, but this gave way to wheeled, half-track and eventually fully tracked vehicles as the swift movement of Germany's panzer divisions was observed.

The M10 Gun Motor Carriage, with its Sherman-based fully tracked chassis, provided the Army with a reasonably mobile tank destroyer, but its 3-inch gun, while a marked improvement over earlier weapons, lacked the knockout power at range that the Tank Destroyer forces wanted. Further, it did not have the speed necessary for the rapid "shoot and scoot" tactics preferred by tank destroyer units.

In February 1942, a set of specifications were drawn up for what was believed to be the ideal tank destroyer, combining speed, mobility and increased firepower. These led to the creation of the 57 mm Gun Motor Carriage T49, itself derived from the 37 mm Gun Motor Carriage T42. These vehicles featured an open-top turret.

Buick was contracted to produce two pilot vehicles of the T49 for testing. The vehicle was to have a five-man crew and be powered by two 165-horsepower Buick engines, coupled together via a Twin-Disc torque converter and driving through a three-speed manual transmission.

While it was intended that the vehicle have a top speed of 55 miles per hour, when the first prototype was completed and tested at the GM Proving Ground, only 38 miles per hour could be attained. It was revealed that there was excess power loss through the torque converter. However, the same tests proved the independent suspension to give an excellent ride.

Concurrently, the Tank Destroyer Command concluded that a larger weapon was needed, and recommended that the second pilot be equipped with the 75 mm Gun M3. The larger gun required a revision of the turret design, and with all these changes a new designation was assigned, the T67.

The T67 underwent testing at Aberdeen Proving Ground in November 1942. Those tests showed that the drivetrain remained inadequate, and the report included a recommendation that a standard, higher-horsepower engine be used in lieu of the twin Buicks. Further, while the 75 mm gun was an improvement over the 57 mm, late in November a new 76 mm Gun M1 was installed, which showed a marked improvement in armor-piercing capability.

Accordingly, the T67 project was closed and efforts were devoted to developing a new vehicle incorporating the many lessons learned in the T49 / T67 project.

The Buick Motor Division of General Motors produced two pilot 57 mm GMC T49s, finishing the first example in July 1942. Since advances in German armor already had rendered the 57 mm gun inadequate, the vehicle intended as the second pilot was diverted from the T49 project, equipped with a 75 mm Gun M3 and a new turret, and redesignated the 75 mm GMC T67. The pilot T49 is shown here during testing with the gun dismounted and a sheet-metal plate screwed over the opening. The vehicle's registration number, 6029910, is visible on the sponson. *Military History Institute*

The T49 had a crew of four. The driver's hatch doors had periscopes on rotating mounts. A ventilator with a splash guard was between the hatches. Two vision slits were on the upper part of the glacis for the driver and the assistant driver / bow gunner. The newly designed 12-inch-wide tracks were steel, single pin, and rubber bushed, with center guides. *Military History Institute*

As seen in a view of the T49 pilot, registration number 6029910, undergoing trials, dated July 30, 1942, each of the bogies had a vertical coil spring for shock absorption. The 57 mm Gun M1 is mounted. The transmission and final drive was rear mounted. Four brush guards are on the top of the turret: two for the fixed periscopes on the roof and two on the hatch doors. *TACOM LCMC History Office*

Although the coil springs of the suspension are difficult to discern in this photo of the T49 pilot, the springs for the first four bogies were to the fronts of the bogie wheels, while the spring for the rear bogie was to the rear of the wheel. A ventilator and splash guard are on the top of the sponson, adjacent to the turret bustle. *General Motors LLC*

The T49 had a flat rear panel on the upper hull, with a taillight assembly on each lower corner. A removable panel was on the rear of the turret. Tests of the vehicle at the General Motors Proving Ground in the summer of 1942 indicated that the suspension system was very satisfactory but that the vehicle failed to achieve the projected maximum speed of 55 miles per hour, being able to reach only 38 miles per hour, due to problems with power loss in the Twin Disc torque converter that the output of the twin series 60 engines was directed through. The T49 did not advance beyond the pilot stage. *General Motors LLC*

In the fall of 1942, the second pilot T49s was converted to the 75 mm GMC T67. This conversion involved installing 75 mm Gun M3 in a newly designed turret, which was open topped to save weight. After initial testing of the vehicle, in November 1942 the 75 mm Gun M3 was replaced by the more powerful 76 mm Gun M1, and this photo shows the T67 in that configuration. Note the presence of four track-support rollers, as opposed to two rollers on each side of the 57 mm GMC T49; also, the bow machine gun was deleted. *National Archives via Steve Zaloga*

CHAPTER 1
The Hell-Cat Is Born

The summation of the lessons learned with the T67 were incorporated into a new vehicle, designated T70. This vehicle would retain the 76 mm gun that had been tested near the end of the T67 project, but in a totally new turret. The troublesome twin-engine power train was eliminated, being replaced with one developed for the ill-fated M7 tank program. This featured a rear-mounted Continental R-975C-1 radial engine coupled to a front-mounted Torqmatic transmission. Both engine and transmission were mounted on rails, which allowed them to slide out for rapid repair or replacement. The suspension was revised, with torsion bars being used rather than the coil springs of the T67.

Buick remained the contractor, and six pilot vehicles were ordered in early 1943. The pilots were delivered in April 1943, with the vehicles being sent to Milford Proving Ground, Michigan; Aberdeen Proving Ground, Maryland; and Camp Hood, Texas, for testing.

Those tests showed that the T70 was a substantial improvement over previous tank destroyers, with only minor deficiencies. Publicists at Buick dubbed the vehicle the Hell-Cat, although in time the name was shortened to Hellcat.

With the deficiencies revealed in those tests corrected through minor redesign, the vehicle was placed into production, with the objective of delivering 1,000 vehicles by the end of 1943. The first production T70 vehicles were accepted by the Army in July 1943, and the annual production goal was met. In March 1944, the T70 was type classified as "Standard," and the nomenclature was changed to M18.

Because the vehicle had been rushed into production, not surprisingly, various changes were made during the production run, including a new gun travel lock and a new transmission gear ratio.

Plans were put in place for production of 8,986 M18s; however, the growing inadequacy of the 76 mm M1 gun against German tank armor coupled with a shift in Army tank destroyer doctrine brought about the termination of M18 contracts in October 1944, with only 2,507 examples being turned out by Buick's plant in Flint, Michigan.

General Data	
Model	M18
Weight	37,557 pounds
Length	262 inches
Width	113 inches
Height	101 inches
Tread	94.625 inches
Crew	5
Maximum speed	50 miles per hour
Fuel capacity	170 gallons
Range	105 miles
Electrical	24 negative ground
Transmission speeds	3 forward
	1 reverse
Turning radius	33 feet
Armament	
Main	76 mm
Secondary	1 × .50 caliber
Engine Data	
Engine make/model*	Continental R-975C-4
Number of cylinders	9 radial
Cubic-inch displacement	973
Horsepower	400 @ 2,400 rpm
Torque	940 @ 1,700 rpm
Governed speed	2,400 rpm

* Serial numbers 1 through 1350 used the Continental R-975C-1, with 50 horsepower and 100 lbs. feet of torque less.

After the T67 project was canceled, the Ordnance Committee endorsed the development and production of six 76 mm Gun Motor Carriage T70 pilot vehicles. The first T70 was ready in early 1943, with the remainder being delivered by July of that year. Early examples had the 76 mm Gun M1A1, which lacked threads on the muzzle for installing a muzzle brake. This vehicle, pilot number 3 and registration number 40128386, was photographed at Aberdeen Proving Ground, Maryland, on June 11, 1943. The pronounced bulge on the side of the turret, intended to give clearance for mechanisms inside the turret, was discontinued when modifications were made to the positioning of the gun. The removable oblong plate on the hull above the sprocket enabled access to the rear of the driver's instrument panel. *National Archives*

The turret bustle of the 76 mm GMC T70, as seen on the third pilot, helped counterbalance the weight of the long gun barrel. Atop the hull to the immediate rear of the assistant driver's hatch are, *on the left*, the hooded bracket for the two fire-extinguisher handles, and, *on the right*, a hooded vent and an exhaust pipe, both of which were for the auxiliary generator. The U-shaped fittings near the top of the turret were brackets that swiveled upward to support a canvas cover over the turret. *National Archives*

As seen in a June 11, 1943, photo at Aberdeen, the T70 had a ring mount for a .50-caliber machine gun for antiaircraft defense on the left rear of the turret opening. A tubular support for a canvas top runs fore and aft on the center of the turret top. The wedge-shaped object on the hull top to the left of the turret front is an air-outlet vent for the transmission and differential oil coolers. Later, this was changed to a flush ventilator. *National Archives*

This June 5, 1943, photo, taken at Aberdeen Proving Ground to illustrate the faulty blocking of the third pilot T70, permits a look at the rear of the hull, equipped with taillight assemblies, pioneer tools, tow pintle, and towing eyes and clevises. *National Archives*

In an overhead photo of an early T70, on the rear of the engine deck is a ventilation grille. A dust cover is fitted over the interior parts of the 76 mm gun. The small fixture on the irregularly shaped section of turret roof to the right of the gun breech is the travel lock for the 76 mm gun. On the rear of the turret bustle is the hinged lid for a storage compartment. *Patton Museum*

The following series of photos documents 76 mm GMC T70, serial number 7 and registration number 40108110, the first production T70, built in July 1943. The occasion was testing by the Ordnance Operation, General Motors Proving Ground, on August 9, 1943. The metal bin welded to the forward part of each side of the turret was for storing foul-weather hoods for the drivers' hatches. Round lightening holes were arranged around the inner part of the sprocket. A good view is available of the 12-inch-wide T69 tracks. *Patton Museum*

A section of six spare track links is stored on the turret bustle. The small, light-colored rectangular shapes on the rear of the hull are decals identifying the positions for the pioneer tools. The gun was the 76 mm M1A1, identifiable by its lack of threads at the muzzle end. Note the weld seams on the turret. *Patton Museum*

76 mm GMC T70, serial number 7 and registration number 40108110, is viewed from the right side at the GMC Proving Ground. Four webbing-retainer straps attached to footman loops are draped over the storage rack on the side of the turret bustle. *Patton Museum*

The T70 is observed from the left side. The bogie wheels were mounted on suspension arms attached to torsion bars. These wheels were equipped with 26-by-4.5-inch rubber tires. *Patton Museum*

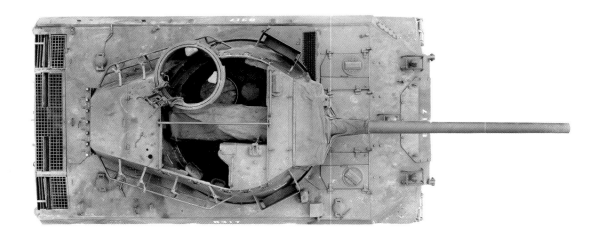

In an overhead view of T70, serial number 7, dated August 9, 1943, the design of the hatch doors for the driver and the assistant driver / bow gunner is evident. Each set of hatch doors had a larger outboard panel and a smaller inboard panel. A periscope on a rotating mount was on the outer panel. *Patton Museum*

Civilians and military personnel inspect a T70, complete with a radio antenna, rolled tarpaulin on the baggage rack alongside the turret bustle, and a Browning M2 .50-caliber machine gun. Unlike the T49 and T67 pilots, the T70's transmission, differential, and final-drive assemblies were in the bow of the vehicle. *General Motors LLC*

A T70 poses along its larger tank destroyer cousin, the 3-inch Gun Motor Carriage M10, demonstrating the advantage the T70 had in its low profile and more diminutive overall size. On the glacis of the T70 is a factory-applied insignia of the US Army's Tank Destroyer force, below which is printed "HELL-CAT," the nickname Buick generated for this vehicle. *General Motors LLC*

A 76 mm GMC T70, serial number 35, photographed at Aberdeen Proving Ground on August 23, 1943, exhibits details identical to those on T70, serial number 7, except the bulge on the left side of the turret has been eliminated. A change in the position of the 76 mm main gun several inches to the right freed up more space on the right side of the turret, eliminating the need for the bulge. However, the displacement of the gun from the centerline of the turret made manually traversing the turret during firing tricky. *Patton Museum*

The door for the engine compartment was bolted to the rear of the hull. Reinforcing for the tow pintle was furnished by angle irons above and below the pintle; these were welded to the door, and the ends of the reinforcements were bolted to brackets welded to the hull. *National Archives*

The top of T70 serial number 35 is displayed during testing at Aberdeen Proving Ground on August 23, 1943. On the engine deck are the armored covers for the fuel fillers for the two fuel tanks. To the immediate front of each filler cover is a round access plate. On the rear of the engine deck are the air-outlet grilles. The four rectangular slots in the grilles are for the engine-exhaust outlets on the tailpipes, directly below the grilles. *Patton Museum*

A chain jack could be used to lower the engine-access door on the rear of the hull. Attached to the inner side of the door were two angle irons, which, when the door was lowered, formed rails on which the engine assembly could be pulled back, out of the engine compartment, for maintenance or repairs. The vehicle was also designed so that the engine could be removed from its compartment through an opening in the engine deck. *National Archives*

The T70s, insofar as can be determined by an examination of photographs and test reports, lacked a stock aperture on the rear engine compartment door for a hand crank for manually starting the engine. This T70, photographed during testing by the Tank Destroyer Board at Camp Hood, Texas, on November 22, 1943, had as a modification an aperture welded to the door, with a plug on a retainer chain. *National Archives*

The 76 mm GMC T70 was standardized as the 76 mm GMC M18 in March 1944. This example, serial number 726, was photographed during evaluations by the Ordnance Operation, Engineering Standards Vehicle Laboratory, Detroit, on April 28, 1944. It is equipped with a partial sand shield; shields to span between the forward and rear skirt sections were not used. The main weapon is the 76 mm Gun M1A1, which lacked provisions for a muzzle brake. *Patton Museum*

The same M18 is viewed from the right side on April 28, 1944, with a measuring rod positioned to the rear of the vehicle. The foul-weather hood and windshield for the assistant driver are stored in the bin on the side of the turret. It was very unusual to see T70s or M18s without the dust cover installed over the mantlet. *TACOM LCMC History Office*

As seen in a June 16, 1944, photo of M18 serial number 1709 during testing at Aberdeen Proving Ground, by now these vehicles had a stock access cover for the aperture for the engine hand crank. This is seen here near the top center of the rear engine-access door. Stored on the left sponson are a three-section bore-cleaning staff and a crowbar. *Patton Museum*

M18 serial number 1709 is viewed from above at Aberdeen Proving Ground. A dust cover is installed over the .50-caliber machine gun. A machine gun tripod is stored on the right side of the engine deck. *Patton Museum*

The tarpaulin is erected over the turret of M18 serial number 2508, photographed by the Ordnance Operation, General Motors Proving Ground, Detroit, on November 7, 1944. The outline of the access door on the front of the hull, for pulling out the transmission and final drive, is apparent. *Patton Museum*

In a view of an M18, the square metal object on the mantlet, surrounded by the dust cover, is an armored flap for the gunner's sight aperture. Bedrolls are stored on the rack on the turret bustle, and the driver's foul-weather hood and windshield assembly is in the bin on the side of the turret. *Patton Museum*

Power for the 76 mm GMC M18 was provided by the Continental R-975C-4 radial engine, an example of which is shown here during endurance tests at Aberdeen Proving Ground in July 1944. To the left is the rear of the engine, including the exhaust manifold and engine accessories, and to the right is the front of the engine, with a ring-shaped oil cooler positioned around the engine output. *National Archives*

Buick Motor Division maintained as a training aid this T70 hull section with the armor removed. The finned object in the foreground is the differential oil cooler, to the left of which are the driveshaft and the outlet duct for the transmission and differential oil coolers. To the front of the hull are the instrument panel, the driver's and assistant driver's seats, the Torqmatic transmission, the controlled differential, and the final drive. *General Motors LLC*

This sectionalized T70 at Buick Motor Division includes the turret and the center and rear parts of the hull, with the front end cut off from the rear of the drivers' hatches forward. The large, round object in the hull is the torque converter, on the bottom of which are its two mounting supports. The light-colored object in the right sponson is the fuel tank for the auxiliary generator, capacity 5 gallons. *General Motors LLC*

The following series of photographs was taken to document the fabrication of 76 mm GMC T70 hulls at the General Motors Truck and Coach Division, Pontiac, Michigan. The completed hulls were transported to the Buick plant for final assembly. Here, a welder is fabricating a glacis assembly. The glacis had ½-inch armor, with a large opening for accessing the differential and final drive. *General Motors LLC*

Workers are checking the straightness of a lower side hull plate for a T70. More of these plates are stacked to the right. These were made of ½-inch armor. *General Motors LLC*

A GM machinist is drilling bolt holes in a lower side plate for mounting the idler assembly, or, as designated in the M18 technical manual, the rear compensator. The holes for the final drive already have been bored on the opposite end of this plate. *General Motors LLC*

On these hull side plates mounted upside down on jigs, the sponson bottom plates, made of 3/16-inch mild steel, and the main upper-hull side plate, of ½-inch armor, have been welded. These plates as seen here represent the interior of the hull. On the hull side plate, note the cutouts for the suspension arms and the reinforcing plates for attaching track-support rollers and shock absorbers. *General Motors LLC*

The joints of the right side of a T70 hull are being welded. The front of the inverted hull is to the left. Partially visible to the front of the hull is the glacis, which has been tack-welded in place. The brush guard for the right headlight assembly has been welded to the glacis. *General Motors LLC*

A T70 hull is secured to a jig, right side up, and is viewed from its left side. The engine deck and the rear plate of the hull have been installed. This jig was designated the first main-assembly jig, and it could be rotated fore and aft to facilitate working on the hull assembly. *General Motors LLC*

A partially completed hull has been unloaded from the jig and is on work stands. Some of the hull plates, including the glacis, the lower front hull, and the triangular piece aft of the glacis, have been tack-welded and will receive finish welds later. *General Motors LLC*

Three hull assemblies are on the factory floor, while another hull is in the jig in the left background. *General Motors LLC*

This T70 hull is in the X-ray jig, where the weld seams will be x-rayed to disclose any defects. Also while in this jig, the hull will receive any necessary touch-ups and final repairs. *General Motors LLC*

GM workers are attending to details on a hull. The welder sitting in the opening in the front of the hull is installing the rails on which the differential will be mounted. These rails will make it possible to quickly extract the differential from its position or reinstall it. *General Motors LLC*

These men are installing the rails for the engine in the rear of a T70 hull. At this point the hull is mounted on a trolley, so that the assembly can be moved from place to place on the assembly line by using the two tracks on the floor. *General Motors LLC*

The rear of this T70 hull is substantially completed, with the engine-access door installed and welds appearing to be complete. *General Motors LLC*

A mechanic is installing bogie wheels. A good view is available of the shock-absorber arms, a bumper above the front wheel, and the track-support rollers. The bogie wheels are brought to the side of the hull on trolleys with lifting mechanisms. *General Motors LLC*

A worker at the Buick Motor Division, Flint, Michigan, is installing the right final-drive assembly on an M18. To the left is a sprocket awaiting assembly, and to the right is the rear of another M18. *General Motors LLC*

With the assistance of a trolley with a crank-operated lift, two mechanics are installing a sprocket assembly on an M18. The holes along the bottom of the side of the sponson are for fastening the front sand shield. *General Motors LLC*

With an M18 hull assembly resting in the background at Buick's plant in Flint, Michigan, a technician sitting in the gunner's seat of the turret in the foreground is calibrating the 76 mm Gun M1A1. The turret is resting on a test stand. *General Motors LLC*

Using a chain hoist, workers are lowering a turret onto an M18 hull. A special turret sling made of I-beams has hooks on the bottom that are attached to the lifting eyes on the turret. *General Motors LLC*

The access door in the front of an M18 hull is open, allowing a view of the controlled differential and the right final drive. The opening in the triangular facet on the upper hull above the left sprocket was for accessing the rear of the instrument panel. *General Motors LLC*

Several M18s are on the assembly line. This and the preceding photo allow rare views of M18 mantlets, which usually were covered with dust covers when in service. These tanks have tow bars attached to the fronts of their hulls and to a conveyor chain recessed in the factory floor. *General Motors LLC*

Buick workers are installing components in M18 turrets.
General Motors LLC

M18s under assembly are viewed from another perspective. To the right are parts bins on trolleys. *General Motors LLC*

Toward the end of the assembly process, the T69 tracks finally were installed on the vehicles. The vehicle's own power was used in this process. The workers at the front of the vehicle are managing the ends of the tracks, to which long pipes are attached. These pipes, which lie between the track-support rollers, will support and guide the tracks as the motion of the sprockets pulls them backward over the track-support rollers. *General Motors LLC*

With their tracks installed, M18s are ready to move to the end of the assembly line under their own power. Dust covers have been installed on the gun mantlets. The mechanic in the driver's hatch of the closest vehicle is installing a periscope holder in the hatch door. *General Motors LLC*

This photo was taken within a moment of the preceding one, from a slightly different position, and shows the same M18s and the same mechanics at work. A man in a suit and holding a clipboard, standing on the second vehicle, is evidently inspecting the progress of the work. *General Motors LLC*

In this photo of an M18 that is essentially completed except for final painting and outfitting, note two bars with ends bent at right angles, one of which is between the first and the second bogie wheels and the other of which is to the front of the idler wheel. These are brackets for securing, respectively, the lower rear corner of the front sand-shield section and the lower front corner of the rear sand-shield section. *General Motors LLC*

Buick employees are performing the final touches on M18s. Subsequently, these vehicles will be painted in matte Olive Drab in the factory's paint booth. *General Motors LLC*

Newly completed M18s are lined up along Division Street at the Buick factory at Flint, Michigan, ready for delivery to the Army. The tarpaulins issued with the vehicles are secured over the turrets to keep out the elements. To the right is Factory No. 01, and to the left is Factory No. 08; the view is facing southwest. *General Motors LLC*

In September 1944, development began on two pilot self-propelled 105 mm howitzers based on the M18 turret and chassis. One was armed with a 105 mm Howitzer M4 in a Mount T20; this was designated the 105 mm Howitzer Motor Carriage T88, shown in this January 19, 1945, photo. The other pilot, the 105 mm Howitzer Motor Carriage T88E1, was equipped with a modified 105 mm Howitzer T12, redesignated the T51 for this application. *TACOM LCMC History Office*

The 105 mm Howitzer Motor Carriage T88 is seen from above during tests at Aberdeen Proving Ground. The ring mount for the antiaircraft machine gun was partially disassembled, and the .50-caliber machine gun was moved to a pedestal mount on the front of the turret roof. The gunner's station was moved to the right side of the turret. Both of these projects were canceled upon the close of World War II. *General Motors LLC*

By early 1945, the US Army had a powerful new antitank gun in the form of the 90 mm Gun M3. This was being used in the 90 mm Gun Motor Carriage M36, but the Army felt a need in the ongoing war with Japan for a 90 mm Gun M3 mounted in a lighter, faster, and more maneuverable vehicle than the M36. Thus, in June 1945, experiments were conducted at Aberdeen Proving Ground with an M36 with a 90 mm Gun M3 mounted on the chassis of a 76 mm GMC M18. This sequence of photos shows the M18 chassis with the M36 turret and 90 mm Gun M3 during tests at Aberdeen on June 27, 1945. *Patton Museum*

The conversion of the M18 with M36 turret was a fairly easy one, mainly requiring elevating the half floor of the turret and the slip ring by 2 inches, a modification that could have been performed in the field. *Patton Museum*

Tests found that it was imperative to use the muzzle brake on the 90 mm gun. Without the muzzle brake, recoil of the gun when fired to the front caused the vehicle to roll back almost 2 feet, and when the gun was fired to the side, the vehicle rocked heavily. *Patton Museum*

At this point in the testing of the M18 with the M36 turret, the vehicle was equipped with the M18's stock T69 tracks; these 12-inch-wide tracks later were replaced by 21-inch T82 tracks. Tests of the vehicle concluded that it was worthy of further development, but the project was canceled upon the surrender of Japan. *Patton Museum*

An early 76 mm Gun Motor Carriage M18, owned and restored by Brent Mullins, and marked for vehicle 24, Company C, 807th Tank Destroyer Battalion, Seventh Army, is equipped with a type of tracks with rubber shoes with chevron grousers of a type sometimes seen in photos of postwar Armored Utility Vehicles M39. *Photo by author*

The same M18, seen from the right rear, displays its registration number on the sponson: 40145937. This vehicle lacks the flap for the aperture for the manual starting crank, which, if present, would be above the shovel and below the small lifting eye. *Photo by author*

Elements of the interior of the turret of M18 serial number 1910, owned and restored by the late Steve Preston, are viewed from above. The gunner's seat, sight, and controls are in the front left of the turret. The 76 mm Gun M1A1C was mounted such that the breech was at an angle, tilted toward the right—the gunner's side of the turret—to facilitate loading the piece in the cramped confines of the turret. In the right front of the turret is a ready-ammunition rack for 76 mm ammunition and storage space for machine gun ammunition. Atop the casing for the ready ammunition and machine gun ammo are the travel lock for the 76 mm gun, and a grab handle. *Jim Alexander*

M18 serial number 1910 wears replica markings for the 805th Tank Destroyer Battalion, 5th US Army, and is viewed from above, showing the open drivers' hatch doors, the storage bins on the sides of the turrets for the drivers' windshields and foul-weather hoods, the machine gun ring mount, and the engine-air and exhaust outlet grill on the rear of the engine deck. *Jim Alexander*

CHAPTER 2

Derivatives

Based on the 76 mm GMC M18 chassis, the Armored Utility Vehicle T41 was developed as a reconnaissance vehicle or artillery prime mover capable of speeds fast enough to keep up with M18 columns. The T41 consisted of the basic M18 chassis with a low, roofless superstructure added on top. Inside the front of the superstructure was a ring mount for a .50-caliber antiaircraft machine gun. *Patton Museum*

The M18 was the fastest fully tracked armored vehicle in the US arsenal. While the high speed is what the Tank Destroyer Command wanted, there was a disadvantage—the M18 could easily outpace the other vehicles in tank destroyer units. Thus, in many instances the movement of the M18 was restricted by those other vehicles.

Addressing this problem, in early 1944 the Tank Destroyer Board removed the turret of an M18 and made other modifications to allow the vehicle to be used as a prime mover for towed artillery, or to be used as a reconnaissance vehicle. Pleased with the results, in March the Army Service Forces authorized conversion of two more M18s. One of these was modified for use as a prime mover for the M5 3-inch towed antitank gun vehicle; the other became a command and reconnaissance vehicle. The two units were designated T41 and T41E1, respectively.

The T41 could accommodate ten men, including the driver and assistant driver, and stow forty-two rounds of 3-inch ammunition.

In June 1944, approval was given for limited procurement of the T41. A total of 650 of these vehicles were converted from early T70s, which had been returned to Buick for modification to M18 standards and included a new gear ratio. Subsequently, the number of conversions to T41 was reduced to 640, with ten units to be converted to T41E1 standards due to a request from the European theater of operations (ETO). At the same time, the T41 was standardized as the M39. These vehicles saw limited use during World War II but more extensive use afterward, including Korea, until finally being declared obsolete in February 1957.

An effort to upgun the M18 was made in 1945, when in June of that year the turret of an M36 90 mm Gun Motor Carriage was successfully installed on an M18 at Aberdeen Proving Ground. With minor modification, the combination proved very successful, but the victory over Japan obviated the need for such a vehicle.

The T41 retained the driver's and assistant driver's hatches, which are seen open here in a November 15, 1944, photo of serial number 4, registration number 9132510. Two shovels were stored on the front of the superstructure. There was no bow machine gun; a tow pintle was affixed to the center of the differential-access door. *Patton Museum*

Racks for tarpaulins and bedrolls were on the sides of the superstructure of the Armored Utility Vehicle T41. To the rear of each rack was a bin for storing the drivers' foul-weather hoods and windshields; this example has the registration number on the bin. On each sponson were two doors for storage compartments. The armor, power train, suspension, and tracks of the T41 were identical to those of the M18. *Patton Museum*

The rear end of the T41 was substantially the same as that of the M18. Two long-handled shovels were stored on the upper rear hull, instead of the one shovel of the M18. Note the lock wires around the hex screws, securing the engine-access door to the rear of the hull. *Patton Museum*

In keeping with the T41's role as a prime mover, the tow pintle on the rear of the hull was mounted on a much more substantial bracket than the tow pintle of the M18. A storage rack is on the rear of the superstructure, and a machine gun tripod is stowed on the rear of the engine deck. *Patton Museum*

T41 serial number 4 is observed from above during testing by the Ordnance Operation, Engineering Standards Vehicle Laboratory, Detroit, on November 15, 1944. The tarpaulin is rigged over the crew compartment. Note the D-shaped, zippered panel below the .50-caliber machine gun receiver, which, when unzipped and opened, allowed a soldier to man the machine gun without removing the tarpaulin. A dust cover is fitted over the .50-caliber machine gun and its ammunition box. *Patton Museum*

In a view of T41 serial number 4 with the tarpaulin removed, a view in the crew compartment is available. At the front left corner of the compartment is the slatted outlet duct for the transmission and differential oil coolers. A tubular crossbar supports the rear of the machine gun ring mount. In the rear of the superstructure is the engine air-inlet grille. Two 5-gallon liquid containers stored on the grille were standard; metal retainers held the containers in place. Two transverse bench seats, front and rear, face each other in the compartment, with the driveshaft tunnel running underneath them. Across the front of the compartment and behind the drivers' seats is the battery box. Note that the left panel of the engine-air outlet and exhaust grille on the rear of the engine deck was hinged, enabling ready access to the engine-oil tank filler and oil-level indicator. This was also a feature on the M18. *Patton Museum*

The machine gun ring mount, its crossbar support, and the front bench seat in T41 serial number 4 are viewed facing forward. Below the ring mount are .50-caliber ammunition boxes, and more boxes for smaller-caliber ammo are stored in the front right corner of the compartment. *Patton Museum*

The rear of the crew compartment of the T41 is viewed facing to the rear. The fore-and-aft tube over the compartment supported the tarpaulin. The backs of the rear bench seats are staggered, with the two center seat backs farther to the rear than the two outboard ones. To the rear of the center seat backs are the transfer case and its accessories. *Patton Museum*

This view of T41 serial number 4 was taken from over the rear of the engine deck, facing forward, showing the engine-air and exhaust outlet grille in the foreground, the stored machine gun tripod, the storage rack, two liquid containers, and the crew compartment. On the engine deck between the inlet grille and the outlet grille is a six-sided door with two brackets on it for holding a portable storage box. *Patton Museum*

The Armored Utility Vehicles T41 were converted from early-production 76 mm Gun Motor Carriages M18, and the T41s were standardized as the Armored Utility Vehicle M39 in November 1944. Above the front of the superstructure on this example is the elevated .50-caliber machine gun cradle and ammunition-box holder with a perforated bottom. *Kettering University*

Armored Utility Vehicle M39, registration number 9113623, is shown in an undated photograph. Above the top of the superstructure is a base for an antenna for the vehicle's standard SCR-610 radio. The doors for the storage compartment on the sides of the sponsons each have two hinges on the bottom, two locking pins with retainer chains on the top, and a grab handle between the locking pins. *Kettering University*

The same M39, registration number 9113623, is shown with the dust cover installed over the .50-caliber machine gun and with the tarpaulin installed over the crew compartment. The driver's foul-weather hood and windshield are stored in their bin to the rear of the superstructure. Toward the rear of the sponson are a crowbar and a mattock handle. *Kettering University*

M39 registration number 9113623 has a storage box clamped to the brackets on the six-sided engine-access door on top of the engine deck. Again, the antenna base is in view above the superstructure. *Kettering University*

Armored Utility Vehicle M39, serial number 19 and registration number 9132525, pauses during tests at Aberdeen Proving Ground on December 14, 1944. Hitched to the vehicle is a 3-inch Gun M5. *Patton Museum*

Armored Utility Vehicle M39, serial number 19 and registration number 9132525, is viewed from the left rear with a 3-inch Gun M5 hitched to the tow pintle on the rear engine-access door. A very close inspection of the photo reveals that the fore-and-aft support for the tarpaulin constituted a hollow tube with an open rear end. *Patton Museum*

The right side of Armored Utility Vehicle M39 with a 90 mm Gun Carriage T14 with a 90 mm L/73 Tube T15 installed is on display at Aberdeen Proving Ground, Maryland, on March 16, 1945. This antitank gun was developed to cope with the increasingly heavy armor on German tanks, particularly the Tiger II. *Patton Museum*

The Armored Utility Vehicle T41E1 was the command-and-reconnaissance version of the T41, very similar to the T41 but with an SCR-506 and SCR-608 radio and an additional antenna, as well as the stock SCR-610 radio and its antenna. In addition to one pilot T41E1, ten T41s were converted to T41E1s for field testing, but the vehicle was not standardized. Shown here is T41E1 registration number 9113623 during evaluations by the Tank Destroyer Board at Fort Hood, Texas, on September 14, 1944. *National Archives*

The two antennas of the T41E1 are in view in this photo of the vehicle under evaluation at Camp Hood on September 14, 1944. A spare-track holder has been welded to the access door on the bow. *National Archives*

The T41E1 is viewed from above at Camp Hood. On the rear of the crew compartment, outboard of each stored 5-gallon liquid container is a storage box with a lid made of diamond-tread plate. Although difficult to discern, the right antenna is to the immediate right of the crossbar that supports the rear of the ring mount; directly to the front of that antenna is the armored cover for the fuel filler for the auxiliary generator. *National Archives*

Whereas the Armored Utility Vehicle T41/M39 had a crew of ten, including the driver and the assistant driver, the T41E1 had a maximum crew capacity of nine. As seen in this overhead photo of the T41E1 during evaluations at Camp Hood on September 14, 1944, various sizes of crews were used. In this example, in addition to the two drivers, there are five people in the command party seated in the crew compartment: three in the rear bench seat and two in the front seat, with a map chart between them. *National Archives*

A 2.36-inch "bazooka" rocket launcher was part of the defensive armaments of the T41E1; its storage location was in the rear of the crew compartment, as seen in this photo of the vehicle being evaluated at Camp Hood. Also in view are two radio sets: the SCR-506 on the right side of the photo and the SCR-608 on the left. In the foreground is the rear of the ring mount. *National Archives*

In a view of the front right corner of the crew compartment of the T41E1 at Camp Hood in September 1944, to the right is the Homelight auxiliary generator, to the front (*left in the photo*) of which is an extra dome light installed during the evaluations to make it easier to shut off the generator during nighttime operations. *National Archives*

During their service in the Korean War, the 72nd Tank Battalion, 2nd Infantry Division, converted a number of Armored Utility Vehicles M39 to self-propelled 81 mm mortar carriers. This example was photographed in the field in Korea on March 21, 1952. Note the two M1 carbines stored on the front of the superstructure. *National Archives*

The ball on the base of the 81 mm mortar was mounted in a socket on a bracket welded to the rear wall of the crew compartment. *National Archives*

The bipod of the 81 mm mortar in the converted M39 mortar carrier rested on an arch-shaped support in the crew compartment. This support straddled the driveshaft tunnel. *National Archives*

The Self-Propelled Flamethrower T65 was a postwar project that resulted in two pilots. Based on the chassis of the Armored Utility Vehicle M39, the T65 was armed with the Canadian Iroquois flamethrower, with a traverse of 30 degrees to each side of the centerline and elevation of +25 to −15 degrees. The crew compartment had a roof with a cupola that included a machine gun mount. The example depicted here was registration number 9132534. *TACOM LCMC History Office*

The same T65 shown in the preceding photo is viewed from the left side. Tests at Aberdeen Proving Ground in September and October 1952 showed that the T65, with its thin armor, would have been very vulnerable to enemy fire, and the project was canceled. *TACOM LCMC History Office*

This Armored Utility Vehicle M39 was photographed while undergoing restoration. Presumably because of the rarity of the original tracks, in the postwar era new tracks with rubber shoes with chevron grousers replaced the original-issue tracks. Corresponding sprockets also were installed.

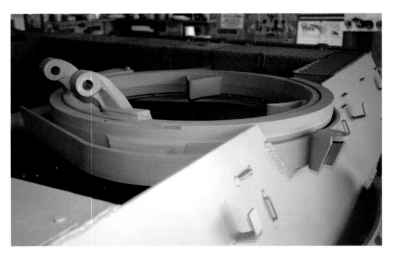

The machine gun ring mount on the M39 is seen from the right front of the superstructure. In the background on the left side of the superstructure are storage compartments with diamond-tread lids. *Chris Hughes*

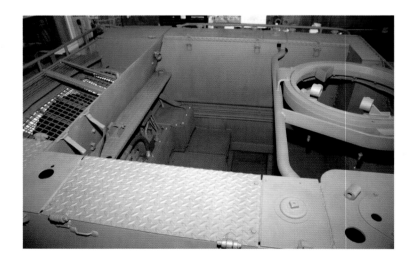

The crew compartment of the M39 is viewed from the right side, showing the ring mount and its tubular rear support, the front and rear bench seats, and, *to the left*, the engine-air inlet grille. *Chris Hughes*

The left side of the crew compartment of the M39 is shown in detail. Note the vertical grille made of expanded steel mesh under the front bench seat, and the latches for the storage compartment lids. *Chris Hughes*

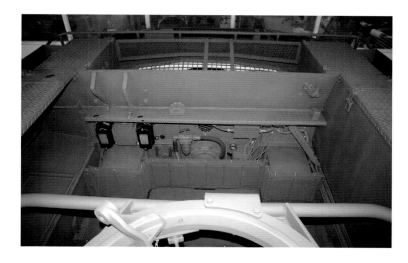

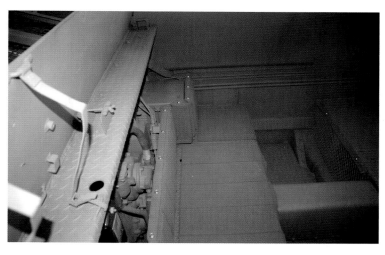

In a view of the rear of the M39's crew compartment, the black boxes to the left are the two voltage regulators for the engine and the auxiliary generator. Behind the seat back at the center is part of the transfer case. *Chris Hughes*

The rear bench seat, the driveshaft tunnel, and the rear bulkhead of the crew compartment (*left*) are viewed from the right side of the M39. Again, the upper front of the transfer case is in view on the rear bulkhead. The transfer case served to transmit power from the engine's output down to the driveshaft, which was on a lower level than the output. *Chris Hughes*

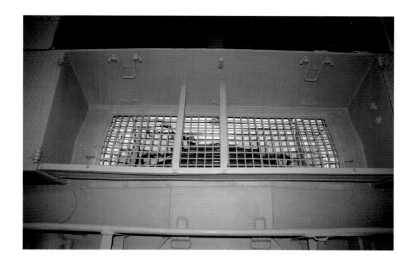

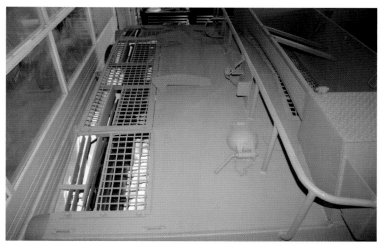

As seen from above the engine deck (*bottom*), facing forward, to the rear of the crew compartment is an open-topped enclosure, with the engine-air intake grille at the bottom. On the front bulkhead of this enclosure are two swiveling supports for the tarpaulin that was rigged over the crew compartment during foul weather. *Chris Hughes*

As seen from the right side of the M39, a baggage rack is to the rear of the superstructure. On the engine deck are armored fuel-filler caps, brackets for holding a storage box, and the grille for the engine-air and exhaust outlet. *Chris Hughes*

CHAPTER 3

Field Use

The 76 mm GMC M18 first saw combat at Anzio, Italy, in May 1944. This example was assigned to the Reconnaissance Company, 894th Tank Destroyer Battalion, and is marked with a large recognition star with a circular border on the bow. *National Archives*

Model	Quantity	Contract Number	Serial Number	Registration Number
Pilot	6	RAD-563	none assigned	40128384 through 40128389
M18	1,000	T-6641	1 through 1000	40108110 through 40109109
M18	1,507	T-9167	1007 through 2513	40114883 through 40146389
T41	2	RAD-2147	1 through 2	9113622 through 9113623
T41/M39	640	T-14346	3 through 642	9132509 through 9133148

The Hell-Cat first saw combat at Anzio, Italy, and thereafter was used throughout the European campaign. In addition to their intended role as tank hunters, the vehicles were also widely used in direct support of infantry. The peak usage of the vehicle in Europe was in March 1945, when 540 M18s were in theater. These vehicles accounted for the destruction of 526 enemy armored vehicles, at the loss of 216 of the type.

The type was also used in the Pacific, particularly in the Philippines and Okinawa.

During World War II, the M18 was used almost exclusively by the US Army. The US Marines received none of the vehicles, and only two were transferred to the United Kingdom and five to Russia under the Lend-Lease Act.

Despite the disbanding of the US Tank Destroyer Command, the M18 remained a potent fighting vehicle. In the late 1940s and 1950s, surplus M18s were supplied to friendly nations, including Greece and the Republic of China. Decades later, they continued to soldier on, even serving into the 1990s in Serbia-Yugoslavia.

Some M18s saw service in the Pacific theater, such as these vehicles assigned to the 637th Tank Destroyer Battalion on Espiritu Santo, New Hebrides, on August 4, 1944. The crewmen are performing maintenance on their equipment; one of them at the center of the photo is greasing a tow cable. *National Archives*

Two M18 crewmen, Tech. 5th Class Joseph Mislausky, *left*, and Pfc. George Kraus, *right*, with Company B, 637th Tank Destroyer Battalion, are interacting with two locals from Espiritu Santo who were permitted a ride on their vehicle, on August 22, 1944. *National Archives*

The drivers of three M18 tank destroyers with the 647th Tank Destroyer Battalion are operating the vehicles on a driving course on embankments of coral on Espiritu Santo on August 22, 1944, to familiarize themselves with driving on this material, often encountered during the war in the Pacific. *National Archives*

M18 registration number 40145192, with Company A, 705th Tank Destroyer Battalion, is parked alongside some bombed-out buildings during the Battle of Brest in 1944. Mounted on the bow is a hedgerow cutter, to assist in plowing through the hedgerows that were prevalent in northern France. A pinup girl is painted on the forward part of the sponson, and on the center of the sponson is the nickname "I DON'T WANT A." *National Archives*

A member of the crew of an M18 from the 603rd Tank Destroyer Battalion has set up the .50-caliber machine gun on the tripod next to the vehicle to cover a side street, while the 76 mm gun is also trained on that street, in Luneville, France, on September 22, 1944. The crewman crouched on the turret is armed with an M1 carbine, while the one leaning against the right side of the vehicle is holding an M3 "Grease Gun" submachine gun. *National Archives*

Three M18s from the 705th Tank Destroyer Battalion, 10th Armored Division, are tucked into spaces between houses in Perl, Germany, prior to receiving orders to move up to the front lines, on November 24, 1944. Parts of the hulls and turrets of two vehicles are visible; the barrel of the 76 mm gun of the third M18 is above the first Jeep in the background. *National Archives*

A mud-spattered and heavily weathered 76 mm GMC M18 is parked in Immendorf, Germany, on December 11, 1944. Several shipping stencils are on the sponson, and "RADIO OK" is chalked above the "CVC-575" marking on the rear part of the sponson. *National Archives*

The same M18 seen in the preceding photo, number 10 from Company B, 827th Tank Destroyer Battalion (Colored), is viewed from above near Sarrebourg, France, on December 13, 1944. The tarpaulin for covering the turret opening is rolled up and secured to the tarp's support bar, and more tarps are stored atop the turret bustle. *National Archives*

A final view of M18 number 10 from Company B, 827th Tank Destroyer Battalion (Colored), near Sarrebourg on December 13, 1944, shows the vehicle from the right rear. A close examination of the photos reveals that this M18 was registration number 40108864. *National Archives*

In the foreground is a 76 mm GMC M18 knocked out by German artillery outside Bastogne, Belgium, during the Battle of the Bulge in late December 1944. Although most of the front of the vehicle is obscured by shadows, it is clear that the front end was devastated. In the background is a Combination Gun Motor Carriage M15. *National Archives*

A snow-dusted M18 from the 2nd Armored Division, US 1st Army, negotiates a sharp curve on an icy road in mountainous terrain near Fisenne, Belgium, on January 21, 1945. The barrel of the 76 mm gun and the mantlet have been wrapped with what appears to be white sheeting, for camouflage purposes, and sandbags are piled on the glacis for extra protection. *National Archives*

A 76 mm GMC M18 is parked in the background as an engineer soldier from the 94th Division prepares land mines at a site near Nennig, Germany, on February 3, 1945. The M18, including its mantlet dust cover, has been given a coat of whitewash for winter camouflage. The main gun is the 76 mm Gun M1A1, which lacked provisions for a muzzle brake. *National Archives*

The village of Irsch, Germany, burns in the background as an M18 stands ready in a field on February 27, 1945. What appear to be two rods have been attached to the bow in order to support a section of spare track and other gear, including a bedroll. *National Archives*

An M18 tank destroyer is serving as a battle taxi for at least eleven infantry troops of the 9th Armored Division on a very muddy road near Lantershofen, Germany, on March 7, 1945. *National Archives*

Mechanics are performing an overhaul on the engine of a 76 mm GMC M18 from the 805th Tank Destroyer Battalion, 5th Army, in the field near Bisano, Italy, on March 7, 1945. The soldier to the left is standing on the open rear door of the hull; stenciled on it is a warning not to drive the vehicle until all of the bolts are installed and tightened on the door. *National Archives*

Technicians 4th Class Michael Sikas and James Leonard of the 805th Tank Destroyer Battalion are working on the underside of a Continental R-975C-4 radial engine that has been hoisted from an M18 for an overhaul. The photo was taken at the same site as the preceding one, but the two technicians are not the same ones in that photo. *National Archives*

Members of the crew of an M18 from Company C, 805th Tank Destroyer Battalion, pose next to their vehicle, number 3-2, in the Baccanello area of Italy on March 7, 1945. The nickname "COVER'S CHERRY" is painted on the forward end of the sponson. *National Archives*

Kneeling next to an M18 from the 805th Tank Destroyer Battalion undergoing an overhaul in the Bisano area of Italy on March 7, 1945, are, *left*, Capt. Swandon, of the 805th, and, *right*, Mr. Joe Andrews, a civilian technical observer for Buick Motor Division, who is wearing a "T.O." insignia on his collar to denote his status. Note the wrecker crane to the left, which is hoisting an engine. *National Archives*

Around the same date as the preceding photo, Buick technical observer Joe Andrews and 1st Lt. Robert Lewis, S-2 (intelligence officer) of the 805th Tank Destroyer Battalion, inspect a 76 mm GMC M18, number 11, from Company C of the 805th, knocked out by German forces in the Formichi area of Italy. At the time the photo was taken, the vehicle was still under enemy observation. Both tracks and both idlers have been blown off. Note the thin piece of steel or armor over the spare track section on the rear of the turret bustle. *National Archives*

A 76 mm GM M18 in the foreground and another one to its rear are firing at Japanese positions in the hills between Baguio and Banangan on Luzon, in the Philippine Islands, on April 16, 1945. These Hell-Cats were serving with Company B, 637th Tank Destroyer Battalion. A rack consisting of a pipe or rod has been mounted above the glacis, and the crew's field packs are hanging from it. *National Archives*

Late in World War II, muzzle brakes finally became increasingly available for the M18s armed with the 76 mm Gun M1A1C, which, unlike the M1A1 version of the gun, was threaded on the muzzle end of the barrel for a muzzle brake. This M18 from the US 1st Army, advancing through Düsseldorf, Germany, on April 17, 1945, is equipped with a muzzle brake. What appears to be a wooden slat has been secured to the bow to help support crew equipment stored on the glacis. *National Archives*

M18s of the 612th Tank Destroyer Battalion are spread out on a street, awaiting orders to advance, while supporting troops from the 23rd Infantry Regiment, 2nd Infantry Division, in Leipzig, Germany, on April 18, 1945. Faded white recognition stars are visible on the glacis and the sponson of the first M18. *National Archives*

As the war in Italy winds down, M18s of the 805th Tank Destroyer Battalion have taken up firing positions on Highway 65, north of Pianoro, Italy, on April 20, 1945. The tank destroyer crews had detected enemy activity on a hill to the left of the highway and were ready to engage. Note that in addition to the shovel normally stored on the upper rear of the hull, two more shovels have been fastened with wires to that shovel. *National Archives*

The crew of the first M18 to enter Bologna, Italy, after the twelve-day battle for that city are all smiles as they pause for their photo on April 21, 1945. They were with Company B, 752nd Tank Destroyer Battalion, and all are identified: Pfc. Henry G. Johnson and Pfc. Calvin Staley in the drivers' hatches, and, *left to right in the turret*, Sgt. J. L. McEwen, Pfc. Charles Dzuiblinski, and Lt. Forrest Holmes. *National Archives*

An M18 is providing support for troops of the 129th Infantry Regiment, 37th Division, during the advance toward Baguio, Luzon, Philippine Islands, on April 24, 1945. When this photo was taken, Japanese machine gun fire was coming from the right side of the tank destroyer. A 5-gallon container and field packs are strapped to the front of the vehicle. *National Archives*

Two M18s to the left of the photo, serving with the 805nd Tank Destroyer Battalion, are waiting with other US armored vehicles from the 752nd Tank Battalion at a clearing in the Revere area of Italy, waiting to cross the Po River on April 25, 1945. These forces would capture the city of Verona on the following day. Faintly visible on the rear of the sponson of the nearer M18 is the tactical number 2-2. Although mud spattered, the insignia of the Tank Destroyer Force is present on the front ends of the sponsons of both M18s. *National Archives*

M18 crews were used to negotiating muddy roads in their drives across northern Europe and Italy, so this crew and riders from the 63rd Division, 7th Army, must have felt like they were living in style when they cruised along the Autobahn superhighway in southern Germany on April 27, 1945. *National Archives*

During the 89th Division's advance through Sankt Goar, Germany, on March 27, 1945, an M18 is engaging an enemy strongpoint. The extra wooden storage box mounted on the rear of the turret bustle is resting on steel channels, which apparently have been welded to the bottom of the bustle. The crewman standing on the hull is observing the effect of the 76 mm rounds on the enemy position. Faintly visible next to the building in the background is another M18. *National Archives*

205925

In the middle distance, a 76 mm GMC M18 with the 781st Tank Destroyer Battalion is rolling along a road into the smoldering town of Auland, Austria, on May 2, 1945. A close examination of the photo reveals that this vehicle had the 76 mm Gun M1A1C with a muzzle brake. On the road in the distance are three more tracked vehicles, including what appear to be at least two M18s. *National Archives*

An M18 with the 89th Infantry Division, 1st Army, is maneuvering through the Lössnitz Forest, Germany, on May 5, 1945. On the bow are markings "1A" for First Army and "60," likely the first two digits of the 602nd Tank Destroyer Battalion, which was attached to the 89th Division in mid-March 1945. An extra machine gun, a Browning M1919 .30-caliber, has been mounted atop the turret, on the right side. *National Archives*

An armored column, including four M18s at the front followed by two M8 or M20 armored cars, has paused alongside the Leica factory in Wetzlar, Germany, awaiting orders to resume the march, sometime in May 1945. The Hell-Cats are heavily laden with troops catching a ride on the tank destroyers. *National Archives*

As the war in Europe reached its end, the 76 mm Gun Motor Carriage M18 continued to fight in the campaigns in the Pacific. Here, an M18 assigned to the 306th Antitank Company, 77th Division, is firing at a Japanese strongpoint at Shuri, Okinawa, on May 11, 1945. This vehicle has as a modification a Browning M1919 .30-caliber machine gun on a pedestal mount on the front right corner of the turret, in addition to the stock .50-caliber machine gun on the ring mount. *National Archives*

A 7th Army Armored Utility Vehicle M39 is patrolling a street in Germany on May 13, 1945, six days after the German surrender. The heavy-duty mounting bracket for the rear tow pintle is prominent on the rear engine-access door. Note the crumpled mud flap on the right rear of the vehicle; the left mud flap had been torn off. *National Archives*

The Armored Utility Vehicle M39 continued to be carried in the US Army inventories after World War II. Here, with a young boy in tow, troops at Fort Meade, Maryland, are preparing an M39 for a run in 1949. The corporal standing in the ring mount is making an adjustment to the machine gun carriage. *3rd ACR Museum*

An Armored Utility Vehicle M39, registration number 9132660, has become mired in deep mud above the tops of the bogie wheels. Recovery of this vehicle is already underway: note the taut cable attached to the left-rear tow eye. The head of the driver, wearing a crew helmet, is visible above his hatch. *3rd ACR Museum*

Samuel L. Myers, the 36th colonel of the 3rd Cavalry Regiment, *left*, reviews troops from the crew compartment of an Armored Utility Vehicle M39 on October 20, 1949. The vehicle has a fresh-looking coat of semigloss Olive Drab paint. Two spare track links are stored on the brackets on the glacis. *3rd ACR Museum*

During the early Cold War period, the United States transferred quantities of its surplus M18s to friendly governments. Here, an M18, registration number 40146106, has arrived at Naples, Italy, under the Military Assistance Program in April 1950. The turret roof and base, grilles, and other components have been sealed for transport, and crates containing spare parts and vehicular equipment are secured to a pallet on the engine deck. *National Archives*

Dock workers at Naples are releasing the sling from a newly arrived M18, registration number 40146097. Among other items, the muzzle brake and the exhaust pipe for the auxiliary generator on the side of the sponson were sealed prior to shipment by sea; the idea was to seal any openings, to keep out corrosive salt and moisture. *National Archives*

M18 registration number 40146106 is being lowered onto a 45-ton Trailer M9 on a dock at Naples.
National Archives

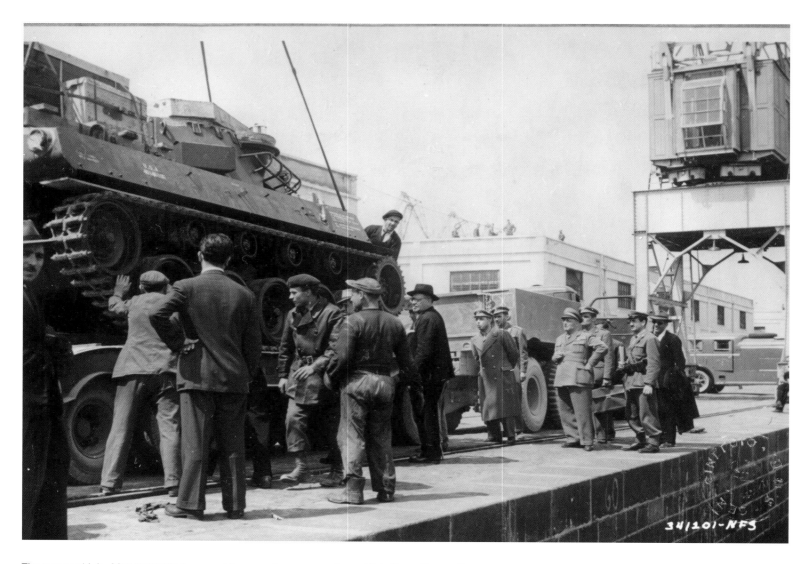

The same vehicle, M18 40146106, is viewed from another perspective, with Italian military officers watching the proceedings to the right. *National Archives*

At a base in Korea on March 9, 1951, GIs from the Heavy Mortar Company, 9th Infantry Regiment, US 2nd Division, are loading an Armored Utility Vehicle M39 before starting out on an advance. Duffel bags, bedrolls, and other equipment have been piled up in the crew compartment. Markings on the right side of the bow are indistinct, but on the left side is "2 R 17." Parked next to the M39 is a Medium Tank M4A3E8. *National Archives*

Members of the Heavy Mortar Company, 9th Infantry Regiment, now are loaded on the same M39 shown in the preceding photo, preparatory to advancing to the front lines in Korea on March 9, 1951.
National Archives

In a photo dating from February 1952, M39 registration number 9132888 bears markings for the forty-fifth vehicle in the line of march of Weapons Troop, 3rd Cavalry Regiment, 2nd Army. Windshields with the foul-weather hoods collapsed are installed on the drivers' hatches. *3rd ACR Museum*

Troopers with Company F, 3rd Cavalry, are attempting a field repair of a thrown left track on an M39 during Exercise Snowfall, a joint Army–Air Force maneuver at Camp Drum, New York, on February 8, 1952. *3rd ACR Museum*

An M39 is towing an artillery piece at an unidentified location. The US Army registration number, 9113623, is marked in large, white numerals toward the rear of the sponson and also in small numerals on the rear storage compartment door on the side of the sponson. "TDB" is stenciled on the forward storage compartment door. *Kevin Emdee collection*

An M39 assigned to the 64th Medium Tank Battalion, 3rd US Infantry Division, is parked along the perimeter of Compound No. 76 at Koje-do Prisoner-of-War Camp, Republic of Korea, on May 26, 1952. A first-aid kit of the type commonly found on tank exteriors during this period is on the left sponson next to the driver's station. *National Archives*

The same M39 shown in the preceding photo, number 23 from the 64th Medium Tank Battalion, is viewed from farther back at Compound No. 76, Koje-do, on May 26, 1953. Enemy POWs are visible behind the barbed wire. *National Archives*

Members of the 999th Armored Field Artillery Battalion, 7th US Infantry Division, are loading supplies in an Armored Utility Vehicle M39 in Korea on December 18, 1952. On the holder for the assistant driver's foul-weather hood and windshield is the emblem of the battalion: two crossed cannons with three numerals 9 (two on the bottom and one at the top). *National Archives*

Troops from the Reconnaissance Battalion, US I Corps, practice an egress from M39 registration number 9132651 to dramatic effect at the battalion training area in Korea on October 15, 1953. *National Archives*

The crew of an M39 from the Battery B, 999th Armored Field Artillery Battalion, IX US Corps Artillery, pause during an exercise at Camp Drake, Saitama Prefecture, Japan, on February 9, 1955. Note the first-aid kit on the left sponson next to the driver's station. *National Archives*

A driver maneuvers a 76 mm GMC across a Bailey bridge. Although armed with a weapon not suited for defeating the very heavy armor the Germans fielded late in World War II, the vehicle made its mark against enemy forces on all fronts during that conflict. *Photo by author*